M000251642

Bulky Knit Wraps & Cowls

9 QUICK, COZY KNITS

Tabetha Hedrick

STACKPOLE
BOOKS
Guilford, Connecticut

Published by Stackpole Books
An imprint of The Rowman & Littlefield Publishing Group, Inc.
4501 Forbes Blvd., Ste. 200
Lanham, MD 20706
www.stackpolebooks.com

Distributed by NATIONAL BOOK NETWORK
800-462-6420

This book is a condensed version of *Cool Chunky Knits* by Tabetha Hedrick (2016), which was cataloged by the Library of Congress as follows:

Hedrick, Tabetha, author.
  Cool chunky knits : 26 fast & fashionable cowls, shawls, shrugs & more for bulky & super bulky yarns / Tabetha Hedrick. — First edition.
    pages cm
    Includes index.
    ISBN 978-0-8117-1648-2
    1. Knitting. 2. Dress accessories. 3. Textured yarn. I. Title.
  TT825.H43   2016
  746.43'2—dc23   2015035669

ISBN 978-0-8117-3951-1 (paper : alk. paper)
ISBN 978-0-8117-6945-7 (electronic)

∞™ The paper used in this publication meets the minimum requirements of American National Standard for Information Sciences—Permanence of Paper for Printed Library Materials, ANSI/NISO Z39.48-1992.

First Edition

Contents

Byram Shawl

Skill Level: Intermediate

The interplay of colors is beautifully accentuated with the openwork and subtle garter stitch texture, resulting in a wrap that is as lightweight as it looks. The asymmetrical shape is perfect for covering the shoulders or wearing like a scarf.

Finished Measurements

Wingspan: 65"/165 cm
Depth: 24"/61 cm

Yarn

Universal Cirrus Cotton, bulky weight #5 yarn (82%
cotton, 18% polyamide; 109 yd/1.75 oz, 99 m/50 g
per skein)
3 balls #206 Autumnal

Needles and Other Materials

• 24" (60 cm) circular knitting needle, US size 11 (8 mm)
or size needed to obtain gauge
• Tapestry needle

Finished Gauge

8 sts x 14 rows in Garter Lace st, blocked = 4"/10 cm
Save time by taking time to check gauge.

Note

• This shawl is worked from side to side in an asymmetrical
shape.

Stitch Pattern

Garter Lace (multiple of 2 sts + 2)
Row 1 (RS): Sl1, purl to last st, k1.
Row 2 (WS): Sl1, purl to last st, k1.
Row 3: Sl1, *yo, ssk; rep from * to last st, k1.
Row 4: Sl1, purl to last st, k1.
Rep Rows 1–4 for patt.

Shawl Body

CO 3 sts.
Row 1 (RS): K3.
Row 2 (WS): Sl1, kfb, k1—4 sts.
Row 3: Sl1, p2, k1.
Row 4: Sl1, p1, pfb, k1—5 sts.
Row 5: Sl1, k1, yo, ssk, k1.
Row 6: Sl1, purl to last 2 sts, pfb, k1—6 sts.
Row 7: Sl1, purl to last st, k1.
Row 8: Sl1, purl to last 2 sts, pfb, k1—7 sts.
Row 9: Sl1, k1, *yo, ssk; rep from * to last st, k1.
Row 10: Sl1, purl to last 2 sts, pfb, k1—8 sts.
Rep [Rows 7–10] 38 more times until there are 84 sts,
ending with Row 10.

Border

Change to k2, p2 rib as follows:

Row 1 (RS): Sl1, *k2, p2; rep from * to last 3 sts, k3.

Row 2 (WS): Sl1, *p2, k2; rep from * to last 3 sts, p1, pfb, k1—85 sts.

Row 3: Sl1, p1, *k2, p2; rep from * to last 3 sts, k3.

Row 4: Sl1, *p2, k2; rep from * to last 4 sts, p2, kfb, k1—86 sts.

Row 5: Sl1, p2, *k2, p2; rep from * to last 3 sts, k3.

Row 6: Sl1, *p2, k2; rep from * to last 5 sts, p2, k1, kfb, k1—87 sts.

Row 7: Sl1, k1, p2, *k2, p2; rep from * to last 3 sts, k3.

Row 8: Sl1, *p2, k2; rep from * to last 2 sts, pfb, k1— 88 sts.

Rep Rows 1–8.

Rep Rows 1–4—94 sts.

BO loosely.

Finishing

Block to measurements. Weave in ends.

Marias Cowl

Skill Level: Intermediate

Long and loose, this cowl features easy diagonal cables that are as fun to knit as they look in the final project. Dress up any outfit with a chic casual effect by wearing it down or double it up for cozy comfort.

Finished Measurements
Width: 6"/15 cm
Length: 67"/170 cm before seaming

Yarn
Premier Yarns Deborah Norville Saturate, bulky weight
    #5 yarn (84% acrylic, 16% polyamide; 92 yd/1.75 oz,
    84 m/50 g per skein)
    3 balls #455-01 Granite

Needles and Other Materials
• US size 11 (8 mm) knitting needles or size needed
  to obtain gauge
• Cable needle
• Tapestry needle

Finished Gauge
15 sts x 16 rows in Diagonal Cable patt, blocked
    = 4"/10 cm
Save time by taking time to check gauge.

Note
• This cowl is worked flat in one piece and then seamed.

Special Stitches
1/1 RPC: Slip 1 st to cable needle and hold in back, p1,
    k1 from cable needle.
2/1 RPC: Slip 1 st to cable needle and hold in back, k2,
    p1 from cable needle.
1/1 RC: Slip 1 st to cable needle and hold in back, k1,
    k1 from cable needle.

Stitch Pattern
Diagonal Cable (multiple of 21 sts + 2)
Row 1 (RS): Sl1, p1, [p1, 2/1 RPC] 4 times, p4, k1.
Row 2 (WS): Sl1 wyif, k5, [p2, k2] 4 times, k1.
Row 3: Sl1, [p1, 2/1 RPC] 4 times, p4, k2.
Row 4: Sl1 wyif, p1, k5, [p2, k2] 4 times.
Row 5: Sl1, [2/1 RPC, p1] 4 times, p3, 1/1 RC, k1.
Row 6: Sl1 wyif, p2, k3, [k2, p2] 4 times, k1.
Row 7: Sl1, 1/1 RPC, [p1, 2/1 RPC] 3 times, p4, 2/1 RPC, k1.
Row 8: Sl1 wyif, k1, p2, k5, [p2, k2] 3 times, p1, k1.
Row 9: Sl1, p1, [p1, 2/1 RPC] 3 times, p4, 2/1 RPC, p1, k1.
Row 10: Sl1 wyif, k2, p2, k5, [p2, k2] 3 times, k1.
Row 11: Sl1, [p1, 2/1 RPC] 3 times, p4, 2/1 RPC, p1, k2.
Row 12: Sl1 wyif, p1, k2, p2, k5, [p2, k2] 3 times.
Row 13: Sl1, [2/1 RPC, p1] 3 times, p3, 2/1 RPC, p1, 1/1
    RC, k1.
Row 14: Sl1 wyif, [p2, k2] twice, k1, [k2, p2] 3 times, k1.

Diagonal Cable

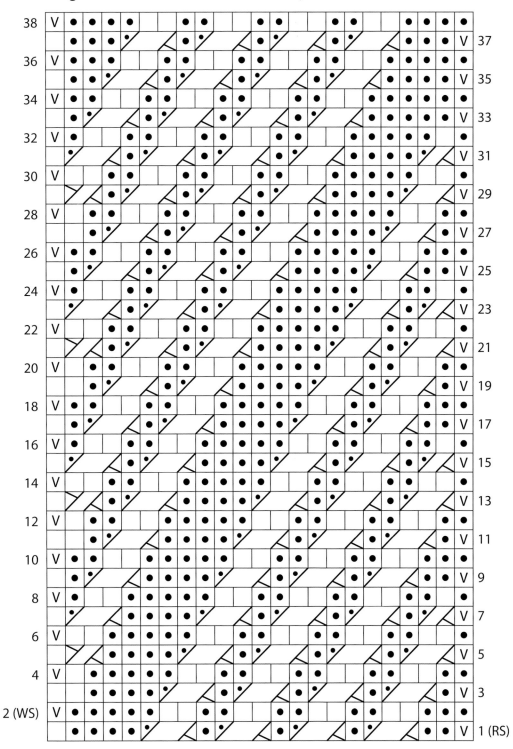

RS: k; WS: p

● RS: p; WS: k

∨ RS: sl 1; WS: sl 1 wyif

1/1 RC

1/1 RPC

2/1 RPC

Row 15: Sl1, 1/1 RPC, [p1, 2/1 RPC] twice, p4, 2/1 RPC, p1, 2/1 RPC, k1.
Row 16: Sl1 wyif, k1, [p2, k2] twice, k3, [p2, k2] twice, p1, k1.
Row 17: Sl1, p1, [p1, 2/1 RPC] twice, p4, [2/1 RPC, p1] twice, k1.
Row 18: Sl1 wyif, [k2, (p2, k2) twice, k1] twice.
Row 19: Sl1, [p1, 2/1 RPC] twice, p4, [2/1 RPC, p1] twice, k2.
Row 20: Sl1 wyif, p1, [k2, p2] twice, k5, [p2, k2] twice.
Row 21: Sl1, 2/1 RPC, p1, 2/1 RPC, p4, [2/1 RPC, p1] twice, 1/1 RC, k1.
Row 22: Sl1 wyif, [p2, k2] 3 times, k1, [k2, p2] twice, k1.
Row 23: Sl1, 1/1 RPC, p1, 2/1 RPC, p3, [p1, 2/1 RPC] 3 times, k1.
Row 24: Sl1 wyif, k1, [p2, k2] 3 times, k3, p2, k2, p1, k1.
Row 25: Sl1, p2, 2/1 RPC, p4, [2/1 RPC, p1] 3 times, k1.
Row 26: Sl1 wyif, [k2, p2] twice, [k2, p2, k3] twice.
Row 27: Sl1, p1, 2/1 RPC, p4, 2/1 RPC, [k1, 2/1 RPC] twice, p1, k2.
Row 28: Sl1 wyif, p1, [k2, p2] 3 times, k5, p2, k2.
Row 29: Sl1, 2/1 RPC, p4, [2/1 RPC, p1] 3 times, 1/1 RC, k1.
Row 30: Sl1 wyif, [p2, k2] 4 times, k3, p2, k1.
Row 31: Sl1, 1/1 RPC, p3, [p1, 2/1 RPC] 4 times, k1.
Row 32: Sl1 wyif, k1, [p2, k2] 4 times, k3, p1, k1.
Row 33: Sl1, p5, [2/1 RPC, p1] 4 times, k1.
Row 34: Sl1 wyif, [k2, p2] 4 times, k6.
Row 35: Sl1, p4, [2/1 RPC, p1] 4 times, p1, k1.
Row 36: Sl1 wyif, k1, [k2, p2] 4 times, k5.
Row 37: Sl1, p3, [2/1 RPC, p1] 4 times, p2, k1.
Row 38: Sl1 wyif, k4, [p2, k2] 4 times, k2.
Rep Rows 1–38 for patt.

Cowl

CO 23 sts.
Set-up row: Sl1 wyif, k4, [p2, k2] 4 times, k2.
Work Diagonal Cable patt until cowl measures a finished length of approx 67"/170 cm long, ending with Row 38.
BO on next RS row.

Finishing

Block to measurements.
Seam the ends together.
Weave in ends.

Apple River Shrug

Skill Level: Intermediate

You'll adore the unique
construction of this
relaxed, comfortable
shrug, as well as how
quickly it knits up.
The subtle lace pattern
works fabulously with
the soft self-striping
yarn, allowing the final
shape to really shine.

Yarn

Universal Classic Shades Frenzy, chunky weight #5 yarn
(70% acrylic, 30% wool; 158 yd/3.5 oz, 144 m/100 g
per skein)

3 (4, 4, 5, 5, 6, 6) skeins #909 Attic Light

Needles and Other Materials

- 24" (60 cm) circular knitting needle, US size 10 (6 mm)
  or size needed to obtain gauge
- 2 stitch holders
- 1"/2.5 cm button
- Tapestry needle

Finished Gauge

15 sts x 21 rows in Wave Lace patt, blocked = 4"/10 cm
Save time by taking time to check gauge.

Notes

- The shrug is worked in two parts, right and left, before
  being grafted together at the center back using the
  Kitchener stitch.
- The border around the shrug is worked when seamed.
- Stitch patterns include selvedge stitches.

Stitch Patterns

K1, P1 Rib (multiple of 2 sts +2)

Row 1: K1, *k1, p1; rep from * to last st, k1.
Rep Row 1 for patt.

Wave Lace Pattern (multiple of 9 sts + 2)

Row 1 and all odd-numbered rows (WS): K1, purl to
  last st, k1.
Row 2 (RS): K1, *yo, k7, k2tog; rep from * to last st, k1.
Row 4: K1, *k1, yo, k6, k2tog; rep from * to last st, k1.
Row 6: K1, *k2, yo, k5, k2tog; rep from * to last st, k1.
Row 8: K1, *k3, yo, k4, k2tog; rep from * to last st, k1.
Row 10: K1, *k4, yo, k3, k2tog; rep from * to last st, k1.
Row 12: K1, *k5, yo, k2, k2tog; rep from * to last st, k1.
Row 14: K1, *k6, yo, k1, k2tog; rep from * to last st, k1.
Row 16: K1, *k7, yo, k2tog; rep from * to last st, k1.
Row 18: K1, *ssk, k7, yo; rep from * to last st, k1.
Row 20: K1, *ssk, k6, yo, k1; rep from * to last st, k1.
Row 22: K1, *ssk, k5, yo, k2; rep from * to last st, k1.
Row 24: K1, *ssk, k4, yo, k3; rep from * to last st, k1.
Row 26: K1, *ssk, k3, yo, k4; rep from * to last st, k1.
Row 28: K1, *ssk, k2, yo, k5; rep from * to last st, k1.
Row 30: K1, *ssk, k1, yo, k6; rep from * to last st, k1.
Row 32: K1, *ssk, yo, k7; rep from * to last st, k1.
Rep Rows 1–32 for patt.

Sizes

Woman's XS (S, M, L, XL, 2XL, 3XL)

Finished Measurements

Bust (buttoned): 31 (36, 39½, 43½, 47, 52, 55½)"/78.5
  (91.5, 100.5, 110.5, 119.5, 132, 141) cm
Length (before grafting): 15¼ (16½, 18, 19, 20¼, 21½,
  22¼)"/38.5 (42, 45.5, 48.5, 51.5, 54.5, 56.5) cm

Wave Lace Pattern

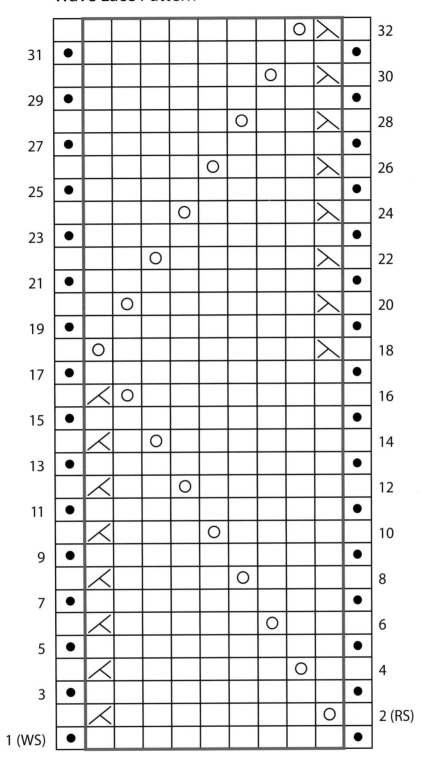

RS: k; WS: p
● WS: k
○ yo
╱ k2tog
╲ ssk

Finished Measurements

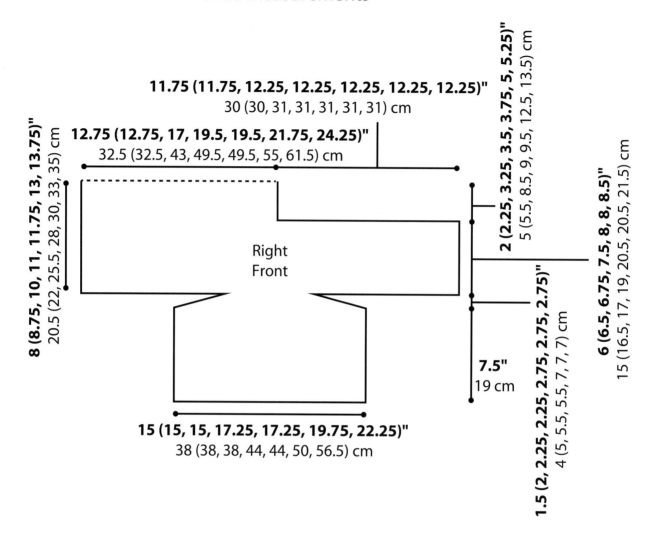

11.75 (11.75, 12.25, 12.25, 12.25, 12.25, 12.25)"
30 (30, 31, 31, 31, 31, 31) cm

12.75 (12.75, 17, 19.5, 19.5, 21.75, 24.25)"
32.5 (32.5, 43, 49.5, 49.5, 55, 61.5) cm

8 (8.75, 10, 11, 11.75, 13, 13.75)"
20.5 (22, 25.5, 28, 30, 33, 35) cm

2 (2.25, 3.25, 3.5, 3.75, 5, 5.25)"
5 (5.5, 8.5, 9, 9.5, 12.5, 13.5) cm

6 (6.5, 6.75, 7.5, 8, 8, 8.5)"
15 (16.5, 17, 19, 20.5, 20.5, 21.5) cm

1.5 (2, 2.25, 2.25, 2.75, 2.75, 2.75)"
4 (5, 5.5, 5.5, 7, 7, 7) cm

Right Front

7.5"
19 cm

15 (15, 15, 17.25, 17.25, 19.75, 22.25)"
38 (38, 38, 44, 44, 50, 56.5) cm

Right Sleeve

CO 56 (56, 56, 65, 65, 74, 83) sts.
Work K1, P1 Rib for 11 rows, ending with a RS row.
Next row (WS): Change to Wave Lace patt and work even until sleeve measures a finished length of 7½"/19 cm from cast-on edge, ending with a WS row.

Shape Sleeve Cap
NOTE: If there are not enough sts to work a yo-decrease combination, work them as St st.
BO 3 (2, 2, 2, 2, 2, 3) sts at beg of next 4 (2, 10, 4, 10, 2, 10) rows, then 4 (3, 3, 3, 3, 3, 4) sts at beg of the foll 4 (8, 2, 8, 4, 12, 4) rows—28 (28, 30, 33, 33, 34, 37) sts rem.

Right Body

Row 1 (RS): Using cable cast-on, CO 32 (32, 40, 43, 43, 47, 50) sts at beg of row, work even in est patt to end—60 (60, 70, 76, 76, 81, 87) sts.
Row 2 (WS): Using cable cast-on, CO 32 (32, 40, 43, 43, 47, 50) sts at beg of row, work even in est patt to end—92 (92, 110, 119, 119, 128, 137) sts.
Work even in est patt until right body measures a finished length of 6 (6½, 6¾, 7½, 8, 8, 8½)"/15 (16.5, 17, 19, 20.5, 20.5, 21.5) cm from first cable cast-on row, ending with a WS row.
Next row (RS): BO 44 (44, 46, 46, 46, 46, 46) sts at beg of row, work even to end of row—48 (48, 64, 73, 73, 82, 91) sts.
Continue in est patt until right body measures a finished length of 8 (8¾, 10, 11, 11¾, 13, 13¾)"/20.5 (22, 25.5, 28, 30, 33, 35) cm from second cable cast-on row, ending with a WS row.
Place stitches on stitch holder.

Left Sleeve

Work as for Right Sleeve to Right Body.

Left Body

Row 1 (RS): Using cable cast-on, CO 32 (32, 40, 43, 43, 47, 50) sts at beg of row, work even in est patt to end—60 (60, 70, 76, 76, 81, 87) sts.

Row 2 (WS): Using cable cast-on, CO 32 (32, 40, 43, 43, 47, 50) sts at beg of row, work even in est patt to end—92 (92, 110, 119, 119, 128, 137) sts.

Work even in est patt until left body measures a finished length of 6 (6½, 6¾, 7½, 8, 8, 8½)"/15 (16.5, 17, 19, 20.5, 20.5, 21.5) cm from cable cast-on row, ending with a RS row.

Next row (WS): BO 44 (44, 46, 46, 46, 46, 46) sts at beg of row, work even to end of row—48 (48, 64, 73, 73, 82, 91) sts.

Continue in est patt until left body measures a finished length of 8 (8¾, 10, 11, 11¾, 13, 13¾)"/20.5 (22, 25.5, 28, 30, 33, 35) cm from first cable cast-on row, ending with a WS row. Place stitches on stitch holder.

Finishing

Block to schematic measurements.
Using Kitchener stitch, graft back panels together.
With tapestry needle, sew angled part at top of sleeves to body.
Fold shrug in half at shoulders and sew side seams.
Fold sleeves in half and sew sleeve seam from underarm to cuff.

Lower Edging

With RS facing, beg at lower edge of right front and pick up and knit 110 (121, 131, 147, 157, 167, 175) sts evenly across entire bottom edge of shrug.

Row 1 (WS): *K1, p1; rep from * to last st, k1.
Row 2 (RS): K2, *p1, k1; rep from * to last st, k1.
Rep Rows 1–2 until band measures 2"/5 cm.
BO loosely.

Front Edging

With RS facing, beg at lower edge of right front edging and pick up and knit 109 (111, 123, 125, 127, 137, 139) sts evenly around right front, back neck, and left front.

Row 1 (WS): *Sl1, p1; rep from * to last st, k1.
Row 2 (RS): Sl1, k1, *p1, k1; rep from * to last st, k1.
Rep Rows 1–2.
Rep Row 1.
Buttonhole row (RS): Work 8 sts in est patt, yo, k2tog, continue in est patt to end.
Repeat Rows 1–2 until band measures 2"/5 cm.
BO loosely in patt.
Sew button onto left front edging to correspond to buttonhole.
Weave in ends.

Calumet Shawlette

Skill Level: Intermediate

Simple lace and soft texture accentuate the delicate beauty of this triangular shawlette. The easy-to-memorize pattern enchants from beginning to end.

Finished Measurements

Wingspan: 54"/137 cm
Depth: 25½"/65 cm

Yarn

Bernat Alpaca, bulky weight #5 yarn (70% acrylic, 30% alpaca; 120 yd/3.5 oz, 110 m/100 g per skein)
    2 balls #3007 Natural

Needles and Other Materials

• 32" (80 cm) circular knitting needle, US size 10 (6 mm) or size needed to obtain gauge
• Cable needle
• Tapestry needle

Finished Gauge

12 sts x 20 rows in Lace patt, blocked = 4"/10 cm
Save time by taking time to check gauge.

Note

• Shawl is worked flat, beginning at back of neck.

Garter Tab Cast-On

CO 3 sts.
Rows 1–6: Knit.
Turn tab 90 degrees clockwise and pick up 3 sts along side edge.
Turn tab 90 degrees clockwise again and pick up 3 sts from cast-on edge—9 sts.
Set-up row: Sl1, k3, pm, p1, pm, k4.

Shawl Set-Up

Work the 6-row Set-Up Chart (written instructions below) once—21 sts.
Row 1 (RS): Sl1, k2, yo, p1, yo, sm, k1, sm, yo, p1, yo, k3.
Row 2 (WS): Sl1, k2, p1, k1, p1, sm, p1, sm, p1, k1, p1, k3.
Row 3: Sl1, k2, yo, k1, p1, k1, yo, sm, k1, sm, yo, k1, p1, k1, yo, k3.
Row 4: Sl1, k3, [p1, k1] twice, sm, p1, sm, [k1, p1] twice, k4.
Row 5: Sl1, k2, yo, p1, yo, k3tog, yo, p1, yo, sm, k1, sm, yo, p1, yo, k3tog, yo, p1, yo, k3.
Row 6: Sl1, k4, [p1, k1] twice, k1, sm, p1, sm, k1, [k1, p1] twice, k5.

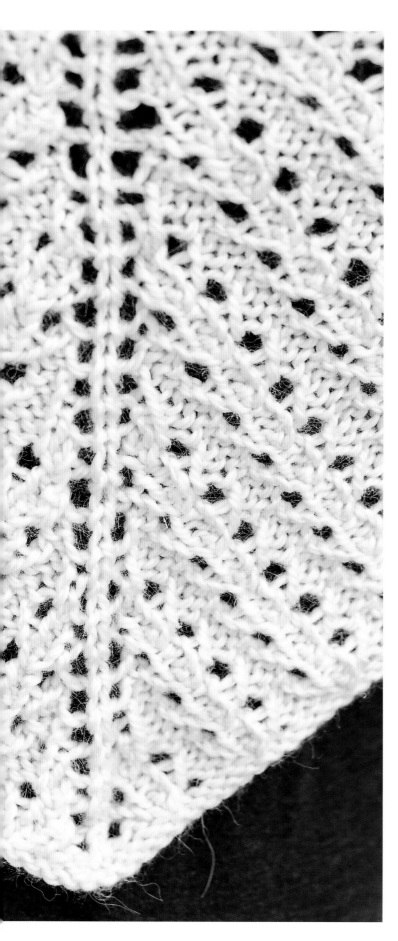

Shawl Body

Rep 20-row Lace Chart (written instructions below) until shawl measures a depth of 25½"/65 cm or to desired depth, ending with a RS row.

BO loosely on next WS row.

Row 1 (RS): Sl1, k2, yo, p2, *k1, p1, k1, p2; rep from * to m, yo, sm, k1, sm, yo, **p2, k1, p1, k1; rep from ** to last 5 sts, p2, yo, k3.

Row 2 (WS): Sl1, k2, p1, k2, *p1, k1, p1, k2; rep from * to 1 st before m, p1, sm, p1, sm, p1, **k2, p1, k1, p1; rep from ** to last 6 sts, k2, p1, k3.

Row 3: Sl1, k2, yo, k1, p2, *yo, k3tog, yo, p2; rep from * to 1 st before m, k1, yo, sm, k1, sm, yo, k1, **p2, yo, k3tog, yo; rep from ** to last 6 sts, p2, k1, yo, k3.

Row 4: Sl1, k3, p1, k2, *p1, k1, p1, k2; rep from * to 2 sts before m, p1, k1, sm, p1, sm, k1, p1, **k2, p1, k1, p1; rep from ** to last 7 sts, k2, p1, k4.

Row 5: Sl1, k2, yo, p1, k1, p2, *k1, p1, k1, p2; rep from * to 2 sts before m, k1, p1, yo, sm, k1, sm, yo, p1, k1, **p2, k1, p1, k1; rep from ** to last 7 sts, p2, k1, p1, yo, k3.

Row 6: Sl1, k2, p1, k1, p1, k2, *p1, k1, p1, k2; rep from * to 3 sts before m, p1, k1, p1, sm, p1, sm, p1, k1, p1, **k2, p1, k1, p1; rep from ** to last 8 sts, k2, p1, k1, p1, k3.

Row 7: Sl1, k2, yo, k1, k2tog, yo, p2, *yo, k3tog, yo, p2; rep from * to 3 sts before m, yo, k2tog, k1, yo, sm, k1, sm, yo, k1, k2tog, yo, **p2, yo, k3tog, yo; rep from ** to last 8 sts, p2, yo, k2tog, k1, yo, k3.

Row 8: Sl1, k3, *p1, k1, p1, k2; rep from * to 4 sts before m, [p1, k1] twice, sm, p1, sm, [k1, p1] twice, **k2, p1, k1, p1; rep from ** to last 4 sts, k4.

Row 9: Sl1, k2, yo, p1, *k1, p1, k1, p2; rep from * to 4 sts before m, [k1, p1] twice, yo, sm, k1, sm, yo, [p1, k1] twice, **p2, k1, p1, k1; rep from ** to last 4 sts, p1, yo, k3.

Row 10: Sl1, k4, *p1, k1, p1, k2; rep from * to m, sm, p1, sm, **k2, p1, k1, p1; rep from ** to last 5 sts, k5.

Row 11: Sl1, k2, yo, p2 *yo, k3tog, yo, p2; rep from * to m, yo, sm, k1, sm, yo, **p2, yo, k3tog, yo; rep from ** to last 5 sts, p2, yo, k3.

Row 12: Sl1, k2, p1, k2, *p1, k1, p1, k2; rep from * to 1 st before m, p1, sm, p1, sm, p1, **k2, p1, k1, p1; rep from ** to last 6 sts, k2, p1, k3.

Row 13: Sl1, k2, yo, k1, p2, *k1, p1, k1, p2; rep from * to 1 st before m, k1, yo, sm, k1, sm, yo, k1, **p2, k1, p1, k1; rep from ** to last 6 sts, p2, k1, yo, k3.

Row 14: Sl1, k3, p1, k2, *p1, k1, p1, k2; rep from * to 2 sts before m, p1, k1, sm, p1, sm, k1, p1, **k2, p1, k1, p1; rep from ** to last 7 sts, k2, p1, k4.

Lace Chart

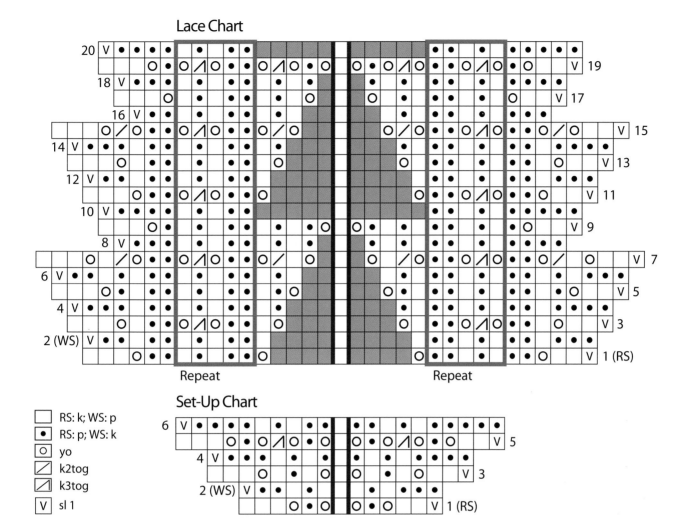

Repeat   Repeat

Set-Up Chart

RS: k; WS: p
• RS: p; WS: k
O yo
╱ k2tog
╱╲ k3tog
V sl 1

Row 15: Sl1, k2, yo, k2tog, yo, p2, *yo, k3tog, yo, p2; rep from * to 2 sts before m, yo, k2tog, yo, sm, k1, sm, yo, k2tog, yo, **p2, yo, k3tog, yo; rep from ** to last 7 sts, p2, yo, k2tog, yo, k3.

Row 16: Sl1, k2, *p1, k1, p1, k2; rep from * to 3 sts before m, p1, k1, p1, sm, p1, sm, p1, k1, p1, **k2, p1, k1, p1; rep from ** to last 3 sts, k3.

Row 17: Sl1, k2, yo, *k1, p1, k1, p2; rep from * to 3 sts before m, k1, p1, k1, yo, sm, k1, sm, yo, k1, p1, k1, **p2, k1, p1, k1; rep from ** to last 3 st, yo, k3.

Row 18: Sl1, k3, *p1, k1, p1, k2; rep from * to 4 sts before m, [p1, k1] twice, sm, p1, sm, [k1, p1] twice, **k2, p1, k1, p1; rep from ** to last 4 sts, k4.

Row 19: Sl1, k2, yo, p1, *yo, k3tog, yo, p2; rep from * to 4 sts before m, yo, k3tog, yo, p1, yo, sm, k1, sm, yo, p1, yo, k3tog, yo, **p2, yo, k3tog, yo; rep from ** to last 4 sts, p1, yo, k3.

Row 20: Sl1, k4, *p1, k1, p1, k2; rep from * to m, sm, p1, sm, **k2, p1, k1, p1; rep from ** to last 5 sts, k5.

Finishing

Block to measurements.
Weave in ends.

Isinglass Capelet

Skill Level: Easy

Diagonal knits and purls bordered by simple garter stitch draw the eye into the lush texture of this easy capelet. Large and plush, it can be pulled down over your shoulders for those chilly evenings or worn loose around the neck as a stylish accessory.

Finished Measurements

Width: 12"/30.5 cm before borders, 16"/40.5 cm with borders

Length: 40"/101.5 cm before seaming

Yarn

Premier Yarns Deborah Norville Serenity Chunky Heathers, bulky weight #5 yarn (100% acrylic; 109 yd/3.5 oz, 99 m/100 g per skein)

3 balls #750-01 Smoke Heather

Needles and Other Materials

• 32" (80 cm) circular knitting needle, US size 11 (8 mm) or size needed to obtain gauge

• Stitch marker

• Tapestry needle

Finished Gauge

10 sts x 19 rows in Texture patt, blocked = 4"/10 cm

Save time by taking time to check gauge.

Notes

• This capelet is worked flat in one piece and then seamed closed.

• After seaming, the border is picked up around the edges and worked in the round.

Stitch Patterns

Texture Pattern (multiple of 4 sts + 2)

Row 1 (RS): K1, p1, *k2, p2; rep from * to last 4 sts, k2, p1, k1.

Row 2 (WS): K1, *k2, p2; rep from * to last st, k1.

Row 3: K2, *p2, k2; rep from * to end.

Row 4: K1, *p2, k2; rep from * to last st, k1.

Rep Rows 1–4 for patt.

Circular Garter

Rnd 1: Purl.

Rnd 2: Knit.

Rep Rnds 1–2 for patt.

Capelet

CO 30 sts.

Work Texture patt until capelet measures a finished length of approx 40"/101.5 cm long, ending with a WS row.

BO on next RS row.

Finishing

Block to measurements.

Seam the ends together.

Borders

With RS facing, begin at seam and pick up 105 sts around top edge. Place marker and join to work in the round.

Work in Circular Garter patt until border measures 2"/5 cm from edge.

BO loosely.

Rep with bottom edge of capelet.

Block borders lightly, if desired.

Weave in ends.

Hanalei Wrap

Skill Level: Intermediate

When using a bulky weight yarn, leaf lace becomes all the more stunning. This rectangular wrap is no exception! Long, warm, and deliciously cozy, you'll love knitting it from start to finish.

Arrowhead Lace

Row	1	2	3	4	5	6	7	8	9	10	11	12	13	14	15	16	17	18
10	•	•	•													•	•	•
9			•						○	⋀	○					•		
8	•	•	•													•	•	•
7			•					○		⋀		○				•		
6	•	•	•													•	•	•
5			•				○			⋀			○			•		
4	•	•	•													•	•	•
3			•			○				⋀				○		•		
2 (WS)	•	•	•													•	•	•
1 (RS)			•		○					⋀					○	•		

Legend:

☐ RS: k; WS: p
● RS: p; WS: k
○ yo
⋀ s2kp

Finished Measurements
Width: 16¼"/41.5 cm
Length: 62"/157.5 cm

Yarn
Wisdom Yarns Poems Chunky, bulky weight #5 yarn
   (100% wool; 110 yd/3.5 oz, 100 m/100 g per skein)
   4 balls #903 Autumn Haze

Needles and Other Materials
• 24" (60 cm) circular knitting needle, US size 13 (9 mm)
  or size needed to obtain gauge
• Tapestry needle

Finished Gauge
13 sts x 15 rows in Arrowhead Lace, blocked = 4"/10 cm
Save time by taking time to check gauge.

Note
• This shawl is worked flat from side to side.

Special Stitch
s2kp: Slip 2 sts together knitwise, knit 1, and then pass
   both slipped sts over the knit st.

Stitch Pattern

Arrowhead Lace (multiple of 12 sts + 5)

Row 1 (RS): K2, *p1, yo, k4, s2kp, k4, yo; rep from * to last 3 sts, p1, k2.

Rows 2, 4, 6, 8, and 10 (WS): K3, *p11, k1; rep from * to last 2 sts, k2.

Row 3: K2, *p1, k1, yo, k3, s2kp, k3, yo, k1; rep from * to last 3 sts, p1, k2.

Row 5: K2, *p1, k2, yo, k2, s2kp, k2, yo, k2; rep from * to last 3 sts, p1, k2.

Row 7: K2, *p1, k3, yo, k1, s2kp, k1, yo, k3; rep from * to last 3 sts, p1, k2.

Row 9: K2, *p1, k4, yo, s2kp, yo, k4; rep from * to last 3 sts, p1, k2.

Rep Rows 1–10 for patt.

Wrap

CO 53 sts.

Set-up row (WS): K3, *p11, k1; rep from * to last 2 sts, k2.

Begin Arrowhead Lace patt and work even until shawl measures a finished length of approx 62"/157.5 cm from cast-on edge, ending with a RS row.

BO loosely.

Finishing

Weave in ends.
Block to measurements.

Lynnhaven Cowl

Skill Level: **Easy**

Rich texture and super soft yarn come together in a cowl that is squishy, warm, and beautiful to wear.

Row 2 (WS): Sl1, *[p1, k1] twice, p1, p1 tbl, k2, p1 tbl; rep from * to last 6 sts, [p1, k1] twice, p2.
Rep Rows 1–2 for patt.

Cowl

CO 34 sts.
Work Seed Column patt until piece measures approx 26"/66 cm from cast-on edge, ending with a RS row.
BO.

Finishing

Block to measurements.
Sew cast-on edge to the bind-off edge.
Weave in ends.

Finished Measurements
Circumference (after seaming): 26"/66 cm
Width: 9¾"/25 cm

Yarn
Knit Picks Biggo, super bulky weight #6 yarn (50% super-wash merino, 50% nylon; 110 yd/3.5 oz, 100 m/100 g per skein)
2 skeins #25616 Duchess Heather

Needles and Other Materials
• US size 11 (8 mm) knitting needles or size needed to obtain gauge
• Tapestry needle

Finished Gauge
12 sts x 19 rows in Seed Column patt, blocked = 4"/10 cm
Save time by taking time to check gauge.

Note
• The cowl is worked flat before seaming.

Stitch Pattern
Seed Column Pattern (multiple of 9 sts + 7)
Row 1 (RS): Sl1, *[p1, k1] twice, p1, k1 tbl, p2, k1 tbl; rep from * to last 6 sts, [p1, k1] 3 times.

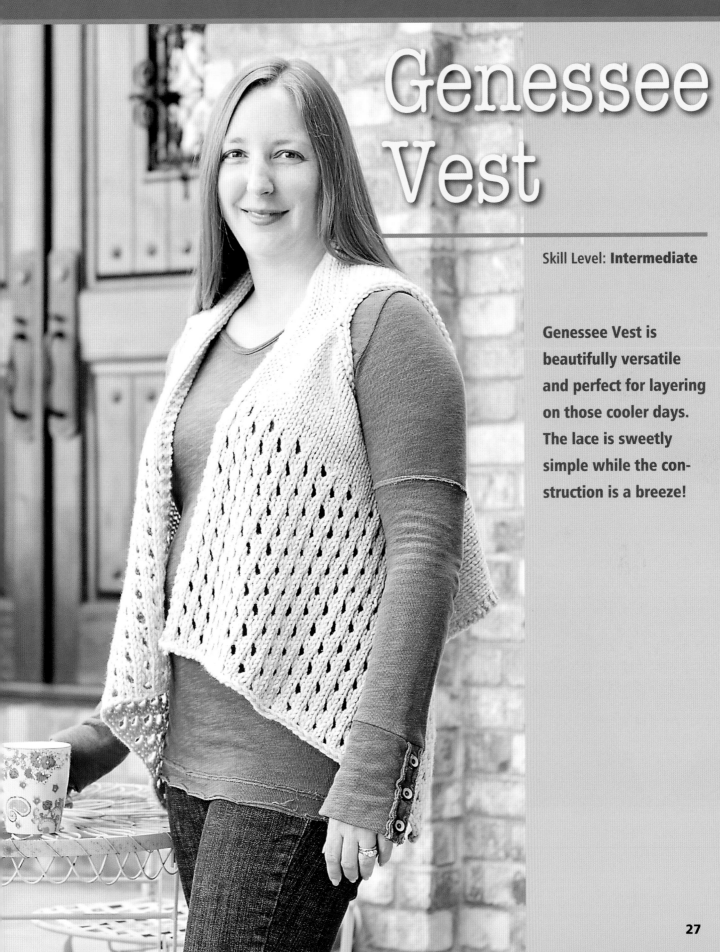

Genessee Vest

Skill Level: Intermediate

Genessee Vest is
beautifully versatile
and perfect for layering
on those cooler days.
The lace is sweetly
simple while the con-
struction is a breeze!

Sizes
Woman's XS (S, M, L, XL, 2XL, 3XL)

Finished Measurements
Bust: 30 (34, 38, 42, 46, 50, 54)"/76 (86.5, 96.5, 106.5, 117, 127, 137) cm

Back length: 20¼ (20¼, 21, 21, 21¾, 21¾, 21¾)"/51.5 (51.5, 53.5, 53.5, 55, 55, 55) cm

Yarn
Lion's Pride Woolspun, bulky weight #5 yarn (80% acrylic, 20% wool; 127 yd/3.5 oz, 116 m/100 g per skein) 4 (4, 5, 5, 5, 5, 5) skeins #671-099 Linen

Needles and Other Materials
• US size 11 (8 mm) knitting needles or size needed to obtain gauge
• 16" (40 cm) circular knitting needle, US size 11 (8 mm) or size needed to obtain gauge
• Stitch marker
• Tapestry needle

Finished Gauge
11 sts x 14 rows in St st, blocked = 4"/10 cm
10 sts x 15 rows in Simple Lace patt, blocked = 4"/10 cm
Save time by taking time to check gauge.

Notes
• This vest is worked in one long piece from side to side.
• Stitch patterns include selvedge stitches.

Stitch Patterns
Simple Lace (multiple of 4 sts)
Row 1 (RS): K2, *yo, k2tog, k2; rep from * to last 2 sts, k2.
Rows 2 and 4 (WS): K2, purl to last 2 sts, k2.
Row 3: K2, *k2, yo, k2tog; rep from * to last 2 sts, k2.
Rep Rows 1–4 for patt.

Bordered Stockinette Stitch (multiple of 1 st + 4)
Row 1 (WS): K2, purl to last 2 sts, k2.
Row 2 (RS): Knit.
Rep Rows 1–2 for patt.

Right Front

With straight needles, CO 56 (56, 56, 60, 60, 60, 60) sts.
Set-up row (WS): K2, purl to last 2 sts, k2.
Begin Simple Lace patt and work even until right front measures a finished length of 13"/33 cm from cast-on edge, ending with a WS row.

Finished Measurements

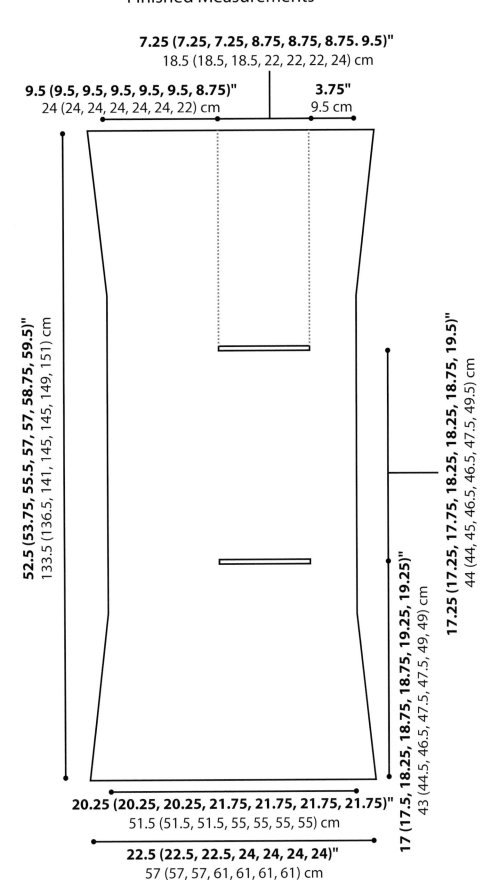

7.25 (7.25, 7.25, 8.75, 8.75, 8.75. 9.5)"
18.5 (18.5, 18.5, 22, 22, 22, 24) cm

9.5 (9.5, 9.5, 9.5, 9.5, 9.5, 8.75)"
24 (24, 24, 24, 24, 24, 22) cm

3.75"
9.5 cm

52.5 (53.75, 55.5, 57, 57, 58.75, 59.5)"
133.5 (136.5, 141, 145, 145, 149, 151) cm

17.25 (17.25, 17.75, 18.25, 18.25, 18.75, 19.5)"
44 (44, 45, 46.5, 46.5, 47.5, 49.5) cm

17 (17.5, 18.25, 18.75, 18.75, 19.25, 19.25)"
43 (44.5, 46.5, 47.5, 47.5, 49, 49) cm

20.25 (20.25, 20.25, 21.75, 21.75, 21.75, 21.75)"
51.5 (51.5, 51.5, 55, 55, 55, 55) cm

22.5 (22.5, 22.5, 24, 24, 24, 24)"
57 (57, 57, 61, 61, 61, 61) cm

Note the edging around the armhole, made by picking up the stitches and purling one round.

Change to Bordered St st patt and work even until right front measures a finished length of 17 (17½, 18¼, 18¾, 18¾, 19¼, 19¼)"/43 (44.5, 46.5, 47.5, 47.5, 49, 49) cm from cast-on edge, ending with a WS row.

Shape Right Armhole

Row 1 (RS): K10, loosely BO 20 (20, 20, 24, 24, 24, 26) sts, knit to end—36 (36, 36, 36, 36, 36, 34) sts.

Row 2 (WS): K2, purl 24 (24, 24, 24, 24, 24, 22) sts, cable cast-on 20 (20, 20, 24, 24, 24, 26) sts, purl to last 2 sts, k2—56 (56, 56, 60, 60, 60, 60) sts.
Place a stitch marker at beg of last row worked to indicate side.

Back

Continue in Bordered St st until back measures a finished length of 17¼ (17¼, 17¾, 18¼, 18¼, 18¾, 19½)"/44 (44, 45, 46.5, 46.5, 47.5, 49.5) cm from stitch marker, ending with a WS row.

Shape Left Armhole

Row 1 (RS): K10, loosely BO 20 (20, 20, 24, 24, 24, 26) sts, knit to end—36 (36, 36, 36, 36, 36, 34) sts.
Row 2 (WS): K2, purl 24 (24, 24, 24, 24, 24, 22) sts, cable cast-on 20 (20, 20, 24, 24, 24, 26) sts, purl to last 2 sts, k2—56 (56, 56, 60, 60, 60, 60) sts.
Remove first stitch marker and place at end of last row worked.

Left Front

Continue in Bordered St st until left front measures 4 (4½, 5¼, 5¾, 5¾, 6¼, 6¼)"/10 (11.5, 13.5, 14.5, 14.5, 16, 16) cm from stitch marker, ending with a WS row.
Change to Simple Lace patt and work even until piece measures 17 (17½, 18¼, 18¾, 18¾, 19¼, 19¼)"/43 (44.5, 46.5, 47.5, 47.5, 49, 49) cm from stitch marker, ending with a WS row.
BO loosely.

Armhole Edging

With circular needle, pick up 42 (42, 46, 50, 50, 50, 54) sts evenly around armhole. Place marker and join for working in the round.
Purl 1 rnd.
BO knitwise.
Rep for other armhole.

Finishing

Weave in all ends.
Block to measurements.

Mojave Cowl

Skill Level: **Intermediate**

Wrapped stitches add a unique effect, ramping up the texture and increasing the knitting fun. Combined with self-striping yarn, the results are charmingly rustic, yet oh so trendy.

Finished Measurements
Length (after seaming): 47½"/120.5 cm
Width: 6"/15 cm

Yarn
Lion Brand Tweed Stripes, bulky weight #5 yarn (100% acrylic; 144 yd/3 oz, 132 m/85 g per skein)
2 balls #753-216 Ozark Forest

Needles and Other Materials
• US size 10 (6 mm) knitting needles or size needed to obtain gauge
• Tapestry needle

Finished Gauge
22 sts x 25 rows in Wrap patt, blocked = 4"/10 cm
Save time by taking time to check gauge.

Special Stitch
Wrap3: Lift third stitch on left needle up and over first 2 sts and off needle, k1, yo, k1.

Stitch Pattern
Wrap Pattern (multiple of 5 sts + 4)
Row 1 (RS): Sl1, p2, *k3, p2; rep from * to last st, k1.
Row 2 (WS): Sl1, *k2, p3; rep from * to last 3 sts, k3.
Row 3: Sl1, p2, *Wrap3, p2; rep from * to last st, k1.
Row 4: Rep Row 2.
Row 5: Sl1, p2, *k3, p2; rep from * to last st, k1.
Row 6: Rep Row 2.
Rep Rows 1–6 for patt.

Cowl

CO 34 sts.
Work Wrap patt until cowl measures approx 47½"/120.5 cm or to desired length, ending with Row 6.
BO loosely.

Finishing

Block to length.
Seam ends together. Weave in ends.